Sinai

SINAI

PHOTOGRAPHY BY Kazuyoshi Nomachi

TEXT BY

F. V. JOANNES
AND
K. NOMACHI

NEW YORK Everest House PUBLISHERS

Library of Congress Cataloging in Publication Data:

Nomachi, Kazuyoshi, 1946-
  Sinai.

  1. Sinai Peninsula (Egypt)—Description and travel—
Views. I. Joannes, Fernando Vittorino. II. Title.
DS110.5.N.65   1981   779'.99531053   81-7777
ISBN: 0-89696-143-5   AACR2

English translation by Judith Spencer

Copyright © 1978 by Mondadori-Heibonsha
English translation copyright © 1981 by Arnoldo Mondadori Editore
All Rights Reserved
Published simultaneously in Canada by
Beaverbooks, Don Mills, Ontario
Printed and bound in Italy by Officine Grafiche di Arnoldo
Mondadori Editore, Verona
First American Edition

We traveled through Israel from October 1977 until March 1978, and during our journey I thought of the title for this book and came to the conclusion that in effect we had visited other regions as well and that, therefore, the title was somewhat strange. But then I realized why I preferred *Sinai*. The Sinai is the land of the Exodus, the land where the sons of Israel received the word of the Promised Land, the wilderness where Jesus of Nazareth fasted for forty days and forty nights. We tried to reconstruct the route of the Exodus, but the political situation did not allow us to start off in Egypt and cross the border between Egypt and Israel.

We photographed day and night; sometimes we did not understand and were not understood by the natives; other times we simply had to hand over the films to people who did not like being photographed. However, we never had any really grave problems. We arrived from Europe by Land Rover, which we had hired in view of the desert, but the roads in the Sinai seemed suitable for other cars as well, even though Land Rovers are more trustworthy.

*

For the photographs in this volume we used the following material:

Cameras:
    Nikon F
    Nikon F2
    Nikon EL
    Leica M3
    Leica M4

Lenses:
    Auto-Nikkor 20 mm f/3.5
    Auto-Nikkor 28 mm f/3.5
    Auto-Nikkor 35 mm f/2
    Auto-Nikkor 50 mm f/1.4
    Auto-Nikkor 135 mm f/2.8
    Auto-Nikkor 200 mm f/4
    Auto-Nikkor 400 mm f/5.6
    Canon   35 mm f/3.5
    Summaron   35 mm f/3.5
    Summicron 50 mm f/2
    Elmar   90 mm f/4

I used Kodachrome 10 for the color photographs and Tri-X Pan and Plus-X Pan for black and white. I often used sunfilters.   K.N.

Sinai

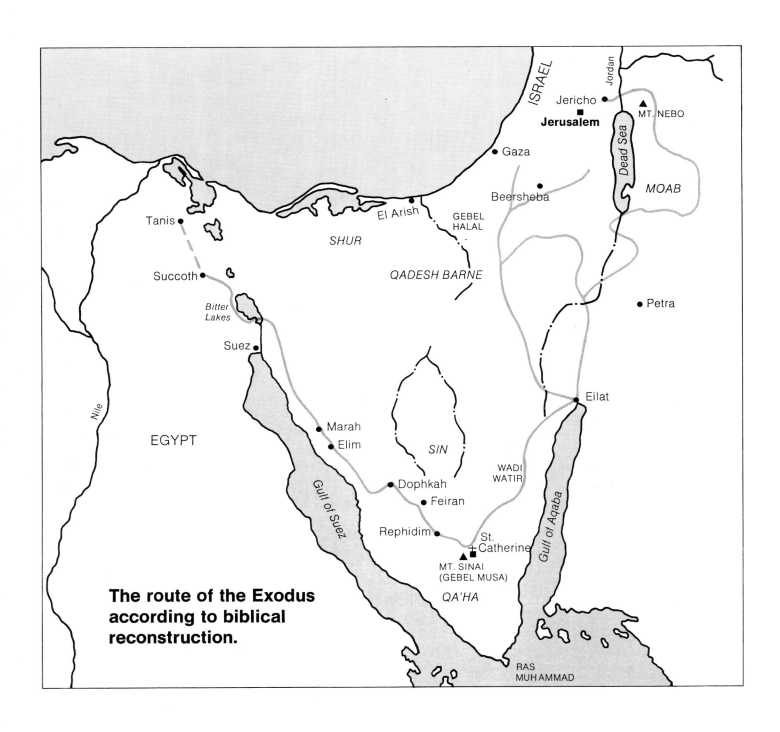

ISRAEL

Jericho
■ Jerusalem
▲ MT. NEBO

Jordan

Dead Sea

MOAB

● Gaza

● Beersheba

El Arish

GEBEL HALAL

SHUR

QADESH BARNE

● Petra

Tanis

Succoth

Bitter Lakes

Suez

Nile

EGYPT

● Marah
● Elim

SIN

● Dophkah
● Feiran

Rephidim ●

Eilat

WADI WATIR

Gulf of Suez

Gulf of Aqaba

St. Catherine
+ ▲ ■
MT. SINAI
(GEBEL MUSA)

QA'HA

RAS MUHAMMAD

The route of the Exodus according to biblical reconstruction.

An Introduction to the Sinai

Many lands are attractive,
But never has the eye beheld
Beauty such as yours.
I know not if the sky bows down to you,
Or if you rise up to meet the sky.

Whoever has climbed the mountains of the Sinai, whoever has endured the burning heat and violent sandstorms, whoever has been up there on Gebel Mûsa, the Mountain of Moses, to catch the sun as it rises in that immense cradle of intense blue, like a river of gold and fire spreading over the vast tumult of rocks, must have recalled the song that Yehudah ben Shelohoh Al-Harizi, the great Hebrew poet of Muslim Spain (1170–1230), wrote in praise of the homeland he never saw and always longed for.

Land of Roots

When setting out for the Sinai, you would do well to bear in mind the advice of Rabbi Mendel di Kotsk: "Take heed that you do not begin to climb the mountain unless you wish to reach the top. Do not jest with the mountain!" And yet the Israelites, a people totally bound up in the Sinai, were told, "Take heed that you do not go up into the mountain or touch the border of it" (Exodus 19:12). When you arrive in this legendary peninsula—whether from the shores of the Red Sea in the south or from the Negev Desert in the north —your first discovery is always the fundamental contradiction of the desert, the oasis, the rocks, the burning sun, or the sudden cold of the night. Nowhere is this contradiction written into the geography as it is here in the Sinai: the need to touch the summit, the terror of reaching it, the conviction that on reaching it, one must leave. As the song of Al-Harizi says, the Sinai is both the buoyancy of the "sky that bows down" and the hardness of the land "that rises up." The Sinai is like Jacob's ladder, an enchanted vision—and search for it we must. Rabbi Abraham Joshua

Heschel said, "Jacob did not climb the ladder but saw it in a vision. So it is for us: each day a voice urges us to climb. We spend much of our time searching for the ladder without finding it. But we have no choice; we must receive the vision as a gift and search for the ladder as a duty."

Each step in the Sinai is at once a gift and a duty, a delight and a test, beauty and discouragement, joy and terror. The Book of Exodus has said all this. Exodus is derived from the Sinai, and not an account superimposed on it, to create a great epic. Together the Sinai and Exodus represent the universal parable of life, which is also a parable of faith—faith of whatever kind: in oneself, in others, in life, in God. Again Rabbi Heschel observes, "Peaceable people believe that faith is the solution to all problems. The fact is that faith puts all solutions into a crisis. Faith is a consuming fire which reduces all certitudes to dust. To have faith means to have problems."

A great faith was released and created in the Sinai, in between the sea and the mountains, in the wadis and oases, to follow a tormented path. It is not a place for "peaceable people"; it is a place where "to have faith means to have problems." Hence the Sinai, viewed here in photographs, is not only history and geography, but a place where for thousands of years the roots of man's fate and vocation continue to hold fast. The history of faith of the Exodus, Moses, Elijah, the Israelites, serves as a basic model for all other history, all other faiths. It was not for nothing that the Sinai became a dream, a testing ground and consolation for Christianity and Islam, which never ceased to feel deeply and emotionally in harmony with Israel. An ancient Hebrew text, the "Canticle of the Sea," a kind of lyric sermon on

9

everything that happened between the Red Sea and the peak of Gebel Mûsa, addresses the Sinai as though it were a living person:

In your streams all fish will leap,
In your rocks all plants will take root,
In your fiery vortex every man will be saved
*   from your peaks.*

If in fact the Exodus is so many centuries old, when one walks in the Sinai the centuries no longer matter. Present and past merge. History or rather the roots of history are as real as events, and in the Sinai events seem like mere episodes compared with the absolute density of the Sinai's eternal history. Its history obtrudes on all other history, absorbs it, shapes it, gives it ever new and different meanings. We shall speak about the past directly, but if, for example, we look at more recent, turbulent events, we realize that even the small number of mines and oil wells along the coast and the inland military camps do not alter that austere countenance concentrated in a kind of vision that is directed beyond the episodes of history towards the very roots of each and every history. This faith that is "a consuming fire reducing all certitudes to dust" has left its traces all through the Sinai, and we shall point them out shortly. But each mark, which is linked to names of places and events, is more of a plumb line probing the deep than a reminder of a single event. The geography of the Sinai has a kind of metaphysical density, which extends beyond geography and history; a density which, when caught in a photograph, is not imprisoned, but moves and breathes, releasing anew that roving insecurity inexplicably drawn to a certitude that remains forever out of reach.

Wherever one travels in the peninsula, with each step Moses and his quest, the fire that burns without consuming, the Face sought and never found, give to the Sinai the voice and appearance of a lost continent forever being sought. If, let us say, the whole of the Sinai Desert were overflowing with signs and objects of a civilization historically and spiritually unrelated to its ancient and primitive soul, it is still doubtful that anyone could disassociate the Sinai from its intrinsic spiritual force.

The Sinai Peninsula is a wedge of land, about 1,160 square miles, jutting into the Red Sea, bounded on the west by the Gulf of Suez and on the east by the Gulf of Aqaba. Geographically it is well defined; geologically it has many varied features. The plateau of El Tîh lies to the north, an immense chalky desert that descends towards the Mediterranean Sea into the Wadi el Arish, also known as "the river of Egypt," and rises 3,280 to 3,937 feet towards Gebel el Tîh in the southeast. Here in this region, a bridge between continents, the key roads of the whole peninsula were laid down: *via maris* along the coast; the "Road of Shur" in the center, which goes to Beersheba and then to Jerusalem; the "pilgrims' road" from Suez to Aqaba traveled by Muslim pilgrims en route to Mecca.

Southwest of the plateau of el Tîh lies a flat sandy area, called Debbet er Ramleh, immediately beyond which rises the group of mountains that includes Gebel Serbâl (6,732 feet), Ras es Safsaf (6,738 feet), Gebel Mûsa (7,362 feet) and Gebel Katherina (8,537 feet). From here we descend to the Red Sea. At the southern tip of the peninsula is the cape, Ras Muhammad, which juts into the sea. Along the west coast by the Gulf of Suez, the mountains are separated from the sea by a desert belt, El Qâ'ah, near Ras Muhammad, half of the

Sin Desert, and the desert of Shur to the north below Suez.

The entire peninsula block is composed of sedimentary rock formed over millions of years from marine deposits. Earthquakes of incalculable force have created a tortured and ravaged physiognomy; other phenomena—impurities such as iron and manganese, the purest chalk and calcite—have colored the rocks ocher, red, and white. Subsequently the combined action of water, pressure, and prehistoric cataclysms has produced a collection of rocks with the most startling variations of form and color. Brilliant and iridescent colors are produced with each rapid change of light in the space of twenty-four hours, and very different tones characterize the two main seasons, the short and colorful spring and the long summer.

Who were the first inhabitants of the Sinai? Undoubtedly the nomads who have left inscriptions in alphabetic characters, to date the oldest ever discovered, known among scholars as the "proto-Sinaitic inscriptions." Some Egyptian inscriptions refer to these primitive nomads as the "gentlemen of the sands," an indication of their haughty demeanor and capacity for survival.

The Egyptian pharaohs from the earliest dynasties knew about the rich copper and turquoise mines in the Sinai. Every three or four years an expedition of 300 to 800 men, protected by a body of soldiers, set out immediately after the rainy season towards the south of the Sinai, returning to Egypt about April or May before the summer heat. The leader of each expedition ordered a commemorative stele to be placed at the mouth of the newly excavated mine. These steles have been found bearing the names of thirty-nine pharaohs, from Semerkhet VII of the first dynasty to Ramses IV of the twenty-first dynasty, spanning the period from 3000 B.C. to 1100 B.C. As well as steles, the Egyptians, who named the Sinai "Ta-Su"—arid land—left a temple to the Lady of Turquoise, located on the heights of Serabit el Khadim, near the beds of turquoise, serpentine, diorite, porphyry, and copper. The most sacred part of the structure consisted of three adjacent rooms dug out of the rock, in which the leader of the expedition slept and prayed to the goddess of the mines to reveal to him in a dream the location of a new mine. The remains of these ancient mines are still visible today; they are still called *mafqah*, the pharaonic word for turquoise.

Towards the end of the nineteenth dynasty, about 1250 B.C., the Exodus of the Israelites took place. From this time the Sinai became inextricably part of their history.

Innumerable inscriptions carved on the rock face of the Wadi Mokatteb and elsewhere indicate the repeated presence of the Nabateans, intrepid merchants from the commercial center of Petra in the Transjordan, who flourished during the two hundred years before Christ.

When Cornelius Palma, Roman prefect of Syria, took over Petra and the rule of the Nabateans in A.D. 107, the Sinai Peninsula also came under Roman rule.

In the meantime the first generations of Christians had created a genuine "Sinai spirituality" by reliving in a Christian light the ancient Hebrew epic of the Exodus. In the fourth century A.D., at the time of the persecution of Decius (249–251), thousands of anchorites went to the Sinai to retrace the footsteps of the Israelites up to the base of Mount Sinai where God appeared before Moses. Soon the large numbers of hermits, dedicated to keeping alive the traditions of the Exodus, attracted many pilgrims, who were followed in turn by merchants' caravans. Thus several towns sprang up, such as the beautiful town of Faran in the oasis of Feiran, which was made an episcopal see in the fifth century; along the western coast three ports sprang up: Clysma to the north, Faran at the beginning of Wadi Feiran, and Raitu, or Tur, to the south. Aila and Asiongaber (the port of Solomon) were founded where modern Eilat and Aqaba stand today; and in the center of the plateau of El Tîh arose the town of Phoenicon, which means "palm grove," modern Nakhl which means "palm tree" in Arabic.

In 305 and 370, and several times in the next century, hordes of desert marauders swept through the Sinai, sacking and laying waste everywhere. Many anchorites were massacred, pilgrims and merchants assaulted and robbed. It was then, in order to protect the monks of the Sinai, that the Emperor Justinian had the monastery of Saint Catherine built in 527 in the form of a fortress on the slopes of Gebel Mûsa. The bastions and great walls, the basilica within containing the splendid mosaic of the Transfiguration, have survived the centuries and still stand today in the middle of the Sinai to receive the growing number of pilgrims drawn by the fecund mystery of the sacred mountain.

After the conquest of Egypt and the Holy Land by Omar in 636, large numbers of Arab Muslims settled in the oasis of Feiran. Many Christians living in the Sinai converted to Islam; those who refused were forced to leave in accordance with Islamic law, which in this instance was particularly benevolent towards the "men of the Book" (Jews and Christians). The beautiful town of Faran fell

into ruin; and all that remained of a Christian presence in the Sinai was the monastery of Saint Catherine with a few hundred monks.

During the Crusades the Sinai came under the Roman Catholic rule of Jerusalem and was given in fief to the lord of Kerak. One can still see today the splendid Frankish fortifications that date from this period on the so-called "Pharaoh's island," or Ile de Gray, near the port of Eilat.

After the defeat of the crusaders at Hattin in Galilee in 1187, Saladin built a fortress at Raitu, or Tur, and at Qal'at en Nakhl on the pilgrims' route, almost halfway between Suez and Aqaba. At Raitu there was also an imposing lazaretto to care for pilgrims in quarantine on their return from Mecca.

Much later, efforts were made to start up the old turquoise mines. In the second half of the nineteenth century an Englishman, Major McDonald, invested heavily in the mines, but the scheme was a total failure.

A change of fortune came with this century and the discovery of oil in the Gulf of Suez, following which the towns of Ras es Sudr, Abu Rudeis, and Abu Zenimeh sprang up; also the ancient port of El Tur came to life again. Another success was achieved nearby with the opening of manganese mines. The recent and controversial Israeli occupation of the Sinai has, nevertheless, a completely new meaning in the whole context of the Sinai. Although the Bible continually exhorts the Jews to return spiritually to the desert and Mount Sinai and the land of the Covenant, they have never shown much interest in the Sinai. The Diaspora facilitated their forgetfulness. Whatever the current political solution may be, the Jews' return to their homeland is also a return to its ancient and still vital heart, to the Sinai. Their return was also for reasons of survival and a policy of a return to the homeland. All this is true, but how can they fail to hear the impassioned song of the celebrated Jewish poet of the eleventh century, Yehuda Halevi, filled with the nostalgia that comes from centuries of exile, longer and more tormented than the exile from ancient Babylon:

If I had wings, I could fly
To you from the farthest corners.
I shall bring my broken heart
Amidst your ruins.
I shall prostrate myself
For your rocks comfort me
And your dust gives me joy.
Your air gives life to our soul.

Land of the Exodus

To bring one's broken heart to the Sinai means to take up the Bible, especially the books of Exodus and Numbers, and the songs and exhortations of the prophets—with their insistent "return to the days of the desert!" To return to the days of the desert is to return to the heart of life and the roots of existence. But not in a spiritual sense applying to all who are not "men of the Book." Here everything essential is linked to a name, a place, a rebellion, a punishment, a penitence, a revelation. To reread Exodus and the whole Bible in the Sinai is not simply a reading of history but a rediscovery of the model for all history, both past and future. The Red Sea and the Sea of Reeds, the desert of Shur and Elim, the Bitter Lakes and the desert of Sin, Dophkah and Rephidim, Feiran and Gebel Mûsa—we repeat these ancient names that evoke the essence of history.

We can trace the Exodus from its beginning, with the departure from Egypt and Ramses, when the tribes of Israel, assembled under their leader and seer, celebrated the Passover and were ready to leave. The Bible tells how the waters of the sea parted and then closed, drowning their pursuers. In all likelihood this did not occur near the Mediterranean but farther south in the region between Lake Timsah and the Gulf of Suez. After celebrating the Passover, the Jews hastened to Succoth (the present-day Tell el Maskhuta in the Wadi Tumilat) and then proceeded towards Etam, ancient Serapium, south of Lake Timsah, where two caravan routes initiate, one in the direction of Qadesh and Palestine, the other to the south of the Sinai. And so began the Exodus; a people lost in the desert, out of which fundamental revelations gradually emerged. They continued south along the banks of Great Bitter Lake to arrive at Little Bitter Lake. In this region, between modern Gebel Genneffe and Gebel Abu Hassan, three sites have been identified, Pi Hakhirot, Migdol and Baal Zefon, where the Hebrews encamped (Exodus 14:2). The miraculous and mysterious crossing occurred at Little Bitter Lake. In ancient times the Bitter Lakes were connected to the modern Gulf of Suez by natural canals and the waters could have easily been affected by the changing tides.

"Then Moses stretched out his hand over the sea; and the Lord drove the sea back by a strong east wind all night, and made the sea dry land" (Exodus 14:21). The strong hot southerly wind, or *khamsin,* is well known to people who travel these parts. Note how elegantly phrased the above quotation is in its seeming ingenuousness. It emphasizes clearly the author's considerable shrewdness, his sense of reality and deep religious beliefs.

13

God uses the elements to complete his designs. This deep bond between the earth and faith will be handed down by the Israelites as a precious gift to those who receive the account of her history as God's revelation.

The site of the first encampment after the Red Sea crossing is the modern oasis of Ayun Mûsa, or the Fountains of Moses, with freshwater springs at the top of a hill in the middle of a palm grove. The water is as clear and smooth as glass; the flora is rich with reeds which are called *suf* in Hebrew. They grow in such abundance along the coast that the sea has been named after it: Yam Suf. Moses gave the order to break camp at the Sea of Reeds and to go into the desert of Shur (Exodus 15:22), a barren wilderness without water, about fifty miles long and about twelve miles wide, flanking the sea. Moses was referring to this land when he spoke to Pharaoh Menephtah and begged him to let his people go "a three-days journey into the wilderness, that we may sacrifice to the Lord our God" (Exodus 3:18). "Shur" means "wall" in Hebrew, and in the Book of Numbers (33:18) it is called by its Egyptian name of Etham, which means "fortress." Here begins, in fact, a long mountain chain that resembles a wall or an enclosed fortress. Perhaps the Hebrews took the name Shur from here, or perhaps it comes from the fortified Egyptian wall that protects the isthmus from incursions by the Bedouins.

"They went three days in the wilderness and found no water. When they came to Marah . . ." (Exodus 15:22,23). Here they were faced with a serious problem, for the water was bitter and the people began to murmur against Moses who turned to the Lord. "And the Lord showed him a tree, and he threw it into the water, and the water became sweet." Marah probably corresponds to Ain Hawara, the first spring on the old road to the Sinai, also traveled by Pharaoh's miners going farther south.

Here at Marah God gave to his people a statute and an ordinance and said, "For I am the Lord your healer" (Exodus 15:26). A mile or so from Marah are the waters of the Wadi Gharandel, which is identified with the oasis of Elim. "Then they came to Elim, where there were twelve springs of water and seventy palm trees; and they encamped there by the water" (Exodus 15:27). Elim come from the Hebrew root *ul* or *il* and means strong tree, oak, terebinth. Wadi Gharandel is the most important river in the vast chalky region. It originates on the plateau of El Tîh with the name of Wadi Wutah and flows for about thirty-seven miles before reaching the sea. The last part, which divides into several branches, passes through luxuriant vegetation.

The oasis dominated by Gebel Gharandel has been described many times by pilgrims of the early centuries A.D. as a little paradise. At sunset the area takes on a flame-red color because of the large amounts of marl; shadows flicker in rapid and fantastic patterns in the brief sunset. One pilgrim of long ago stopped to describe the many small hermitages that populated this site of the biblical encampment. These hermits were the first of a generations-long tradition of men who believed that they were the heirs of the ancient Exodus, as much a part of it as the early participants themselves. The Israelites set out from Elim and encamped near the Sea of Reeds, or the Red Sea (Numbers 33:10). There are abundant springs to be found in the coastal desert areas; one need only dig a few feet to find fresh drinking water. Bedouins today know this and undoubtedly so did Moses. And here is Gebel Hamman el Firuan, formed from calcareous rock, which is perforated by grottos and dotted with sulphur springs. The Arabs, who gave it its fanciful name, which means "Pharaoh submerged in water," imagined that in the strange shape of the mountain they could see Pharaoh swallowed up by the sea!

There are two industrial centers in this region today: Abu Rudeis for petroleum and Abu Zenimeh where the Egyptians have built an industrial complex for purifying manganese. The road passes between oil wells and gigantic storage tanks, and at night the red glare of the natural-gas flames brings to mind in a strange way the pillar of fire that led the Israelites along the way out of Egypt (Exodus 13:21,22).

They set out from this place for the desert of Sin, identified with the vast half–moon-shaped stretch of sand called Debbet er Ramleh situated between Serabit el Khadim and the plateau of El Tîh, between the Wadi Gharandel and the Sinai. To the north the desert is bounded by the mountain chain of El Tîh, which gives its name to the whole desert, for it begins near Port Taufiq, stretches eastwards, and by forming a curve it closes off the region of Qadesh Barne. The desert of Sin recalls two events of the Exodus: the manna and the quails from heaven. In the spring and autumn flocks of quail set out from Africa and Arabia for the Mediterranean countries, stopping along the Sinai coast. They fly low and are carried along by the wind and when they arrive, tired from the long flight, they are easily caught.

There is an interesting explanation in nature for the appearance of the manna, which is given a supernatural significance in the Bible. Along the western coast of the Sinai, the tamarisk (*Tamarix mannifera*) grows often in groves to a height of forty feet or so. Between May and August the youngest twigs swell up, exuding a whitish substance which, when exposed to the air, hardens into fragrant and highly nutritious berries. With the heat of the sun the berries melt, which is why the Bedouin gather them in the evening or early morning, as the Bible commanded the Hebrews. The word "manna" is derived from the Hebrew *man-hu,* which means "What is it?" The Arabs call it *man min sama* or "manna from heaven."

"All the congregation of the people of Israel moved on from the wilderness of Sin by stages according to the commandment of the Lord" (Exodus 17:1). The Book of Numbers (33:13,14) mentions Dophkah and Alush followed by Rephidim. Mafqah ("turquoise"), the old Pharaonic mines in the Wadi Magharah, is probably Dophkah; and Magharah, meaning "cave," would be about five miles of underground mines. The presence of this Egyptian temple on the heights of Serabit el Khadim, dedicated to the Lady of Turquoise, goddess of the mines, allows a more accurate identification of the references in the Book of Exodus. From its elevated position—unusual for Egyptian religious architecture—this temple, one of the holiest in Egypt, overlooked the desert and the road leading to Mafqah. The road lay within Egyptian territory and was therefore reasonably safe for travelers leaving Egypt for the east. For this reason the Israelites could advance along this road, and it was not until they had left Rephidim and passed out of Egyptian territory that they were attacked from the rear by the Amalekites.

The other Biblical town, Alush, between Dophkah and Rephidim, may have been situated in the Wadi Mokatteb, the valley of inscriptions; in fact, its name means "inscription valley." Rocks which were once part of the granite and calceous walls bear thousands of inscriptions made by Nabatean, Greek, Arab, Roman, and Syrian pilgrims who made their way here by camel. On arriving at Rephidim (identified with the large Wadi Rephaid), Moses struck the rock with his rod and the water came forth fresh and abundant (Exodus 17:2–7). According to Hebrew legend, the rock from which the water gushed forth always accompanied the people in the desert. What was once legend soon became a point of great theological importance, as did all the events of the Exodus. Rabbinical scholars studying numerous biblical texts in which God is called "the rock of Israel" see in this rock the presence of God himself among his people. And Saint Paul boldly synthesised the ancient Exodus and contemporary events: "For they drank from the supernatural Rock which followed them, and the Rock was Christ" (1 Corinthians 10:4).

The Bedouins have designated a rock in Hesi el Khattatin as the one from which Moses made water appear. Every time they pass by Hesi el Khattatin, which in Arabic means "hidden spring," they place a stone there. Moses named this place Massah and Meribah because of a dispute among the children of Israel and because they had put God to the test, saying, "Is the Lord among us or not?" Massah means "temptation"; Meribah means "place of disputes." The exact historical site is in any case of little importance. Clearly the author of the Book of Exodus intended to give a more universal significance to individual events. The writer of Psalm 95 exhorts the pilgrims going

to Jerusalem to show docility to God and reminds them of these two places, famous for the quarrels of the Israelites, a symbol of the struggle between the God and the people of the Exodus, a symbol of a religion that points out the fundamental structure in the concept of a continuous exodus.

Land of Strife

Each stage of the Exodus into the Sinai is indeed synonymous with strife: strife with nature, capricious and unexpectedly avaricious or generous; strife with oneself and with others when the desert draws in, harsh and inhospitable; strife with God when his designs seem totally unreasonable. Freud found abundant material for analysis in the Exodus and in the figure of Moses.

There were precise moments of strife, as at Feiran, for example, the most beautiful oasis of the Sinai and which seemed to the people of the Exodus like the realization of a dream nurtured since the days of slavery in Egypt.

To reach Feiran, in the region of Rephidim, one follows the wadi, which is initially like an immense river of unimaginable colors. The rocks on either side are of red-and-black granite with greenish and mother-of-pearl veining. Even today it is a very difficult place to reach and one must have reliable guides to avoid getting lost in the sands or chasing after seemingly shorter routes. Pilgrims from centuries past arrived here by camel and their accounts are full of dramatic incidents. One of these pilgrims, a well-traveled Franciscan Brother by name of Niccolò da Poggibonsi, who arrived at Feiran in 1347, describes at length his adventurous travels in the Sinai. He observes, "One thing is certain, that if there were no camels we could not get to Saint Catherine, the reason being that no other animal could walk so far or endure such a perilous journey, or carry so many provisions." This description from the fourteenth century is still equally valid today.

The oasis of Feiran, which means "the fertile one," is hidden away amid great overhanging rocks. After hours and hours of desert it appears like a mirage. This is the pearl of the Sinai, luxuriant with palm trees, tamarisks, acacias, and aromatic herbs.

Almost at the beginning of the oasis where the wadi widens are a small hill and a garden. Here Faran sprang up, the only city of the Sinai located at the foot of Gebel Serbal (6,732 feet). Together with Saint Catherine and Tur, Faran was the center of monastic life in the Sinai. Here and there on the eastern slope of the hill are monastery ruins, and small churches and cells are scattered over the area. By the banks of the stream that irrigates the oasis stand the small houses of the seminomadic or sedentary Bedouins. They are the descendants of the Christian families whom the Emperor Justinian brought to the Sinai to assist the monks of Saint Catherine, and who converted to Islam with the arrival of the Arabs. Many of the names of the people and places and many Arabic words used today in the Sinai are derived from Greek, the language of their ancestors.

Acacias with small leaves and long, sharp thorns flower abundantly in the oasis. This tree, which is commonly found in the Sinai, was used to build the Ark of the Testament, or Covenant (Exodus 25:10) in which Moses placed the Tables of the Law. The Ark always accompanied the people and was always at the center of their travels and their progressive occupation of the land of Israel; it was placed in the Temple of Jerusalem, symbol of the covenant between God and his people.

The Hebrew people fought their first battle at Feiran. They were attacked from the rear by an ancient tribe of the Sinai, the Amalekites, or people of Amalek, who inhabited the northern region of the peninsula, the plateau of El Tîh. Exodus gives a full account of this battle, in which the Hebrews were led by Joshua, while Moses stood on top of a hill with Aaron and Hur.

Whenever Moses held up his hand, Israel prevailed; and whenever he lowered his hand, Amalek prevailed. But Moses' hands grew weary; so they took a stone and put it under him, and he sat upon it, and Aaron and Hur held up his hands, one on one side, and the other on the other side; so his hands were steady until the going down of the sun.

—EXODUS 17:11–12

Israel won the battle and Moses built an altar at Feiran and called it *Yaweh Nissi,* which means "God is my banner." (Exodus 17:13–15)

It is evident from these accounts that we are dealing with a very primitive religion, whose attitudes antedate the Jewish religion and are derived from customs of other eastern peoples. But the prayer of Moses, traditionally attributed to this place, with its background of Mount Serval and its five enormous peaks of pink granite, became symbolic of all prayer throughout the Bible—a continual struggle assuaged by trust in God who chose the Hebrews for a covenant rich with promises. It is a struggle that saw the episode of the prophet of fire, Elijah, take place in the very heart of the Sinai where the Covenant and the

Revelation were brought about. During the northern rule, when the land of Israel had been conquered and the memory of the Exodus and the Sinai had dimmed, the people of the Covenant turned to idolatry. *Baalim,* the idols of other eastern religions, were being worshiped in temples by the people who had received the revelation of their invisible God. After the prophet Elijah put to death the high priests of Baal at the foot of Mount Carmel, he was forced to flee, for Jezebel, wife of King Ahab, had sworn death to him for having tried to destroy idolatry among the Israelites, a practice that she had introduced and favored. Elijah fled towards the south by stages an anguished journey during which he embraced once again the origins of his religion and the faith of his people. He arrived at Mount Horeb, where Moses spoke to God.

The account of Elijah's experience in 1 Kings 19 has a clearly controversial intention: to return to the harsh but happy days of the Covenant. The Sinai represents the end of an epoch and a conquest which must be resumed again and again. On the final stage of the journey to the top of Mount Horeb, a valley named after Elijah appears. There we are reminded of the need for that continual return to the covenant and the enduring principle of the Exodus is reaffirmed.

After the oasis of Feiran the wadi becomes enormous once again and we are back in the middle of the desert. At the foot of Gebel el Bueib, or "the little gate," the wadi narrows and passes through a narrow gorge. The Israelites were probably attacked by the Amalekites here at the gate of el Bueib before they crossed to put up their tents by Gebel Mûsa. After the gorge of el Bueib, the horizon opens up to an imposing view of rocks of every color and shape. We are now in the Wadi es Sheikh which, together with the Wadi Solaf, leads to the heart of the Sinai Desert.

Land of the Covenant

Suddenly, like a vision from afar, the outline of the fortified monastery of Saint Catherine comes into view between the mountain peaks.

The Bible relates that once before Moses came to Mount Sinai, when he was tending the flock of Jethro (Exodus 3:1). In the place where today the monastery of Saint Catherine stands, God appeared before him in a flame of fire out of the midst of a bush. The word for bush, *seneh,* refers to *Crataegus sinaiticus spinosus,* which grows to heights of between six and ten feet. Then God said to Moses, "Do not come near, put off your shoes from your feet, for the place on which you are standing is holy ground." This tradition was respected by Justinian's architect in the unusual plan of the church. Behind the sixth-century apse, there are three steps leading to the small chapel of the burning bush, which of all the places in the Sinai is the "holy of holies." People today still enter barefoot, as God commanded Moses.

The earliest pilgrims were so awestruck by the holiness of this place that on first catching sight of the mountain peaks they fell to their knees in adoration. This group of mountains is an imposing sight. Its oblong shape extends from northwest to southeast over a radius of approximately two and a half by one and one-quarter miles, surrounded by the plain of El Raha to the north and by deep wadis—Wadi el Deir to the southeast and Wadi Legiah to the southwest. From this sea of mountaintops the three peaks of Gebel Ras es Safsaf emerge to the northwest (the highest is 6,739 feet); to the south is the single peak of Gebel Mûsa (7,362 feet), until the twelfth century called Gebel Moneigiah, or "mountain of encounter"; to the west Gebel Homr and to the southwest Gebel Katherīna (8,536 feet), the tallest of the whole peninsula.

The plain of El Raha, the "valley of repose," is also called, appropriately, "desert of the Sinai." This vast amphitheatre, set apart in a multitude of mountains, seems designed for an encounter of extraordinary greatness, perceived by those who long ago gave it its name. Traditionally, the encampment of the Israelites is situated here (Exodus 19:1). From here the people were able to observe the great event when God appeared to Moses. Moses went up to God, who called to him out of the mountain. The words that were heard had a haunting and powerful effect:

> You have seen what I did to the Egyptians, and how I bore you on eagles' wings and brought you to myself. Now therefore, if you will obey my voice and keep my covenant, you shall be my own possession among all peoples; for all the earth is mine, and you shall be to me a kingdom of priests and a holy nation.
>
> —EXODUS 19:4–6

The people accepted the invitation and God prepared a grandiose spectacle within this setting so that all could bear witness to his extraordinary communication to Moses. When Moses came down from the mountain he told the people of the Decalogue (Exodus 20–23), and, to commemorate the event he built an altar, and twelve pillars for the twelve tribes, at the foot of the mountain. The plain of El Raha is remembered for this event.

Moses then went up Mount Sinai again with Aaron, Nadab, Abihu, and seventy elders of Israel and "they saw the God of Israel; and there was under his feet as it were a pavement of lapis lazuli, like the very heaven for clearness" (Exodus 24:1–2, 9–11). Only Moses and his loyal servant Joshua climbed up to the peak of the mountain as they had been commanded by God, and the cloud covered the mountain for six days and the glory of God settled on the mountain. The glory of God appeared to the people like a devouring fire on the mountaintop.

Moses entered the cloud on the mountain and stayed there for forty days and forty nights. The number forty is a conventional biblical figure indicating a long period of preparation. To the Semites the number forty refers to a period of trial and grace, a time for decisive action, and the receiving of divine revelation. The number forty appears regularly in the Bible, as, for example, the prophet Elijah walked forty days to reach Mount Sinai; the forty different settlements of the Hebrews during the Exodus and their forty years of wandering; Joshua explored the Promised Land for forty days; there are forty genealogical links between Abraham and Jesus; there were the forty days of fasting by Jesus in the desert; and the forty days of Jesus after the Resurrection.

The Bible maintains that Moses passed beyond the cloud, and according to ancient cosmology the clouds were part of heaven. In going beyond the clouds, Moses went beyond the present world and entered the world of God himself. And when he had finished speaking with Moses, God gave to him the two tables of the testimony, or Covenant. This moment is the focal point of the whole account of Exodus—from which Israel takes its name as "the people of the Covenant." Its whole history will be decided, both the good and the bad, in the light of this covenant.

Therefore the making of the golden calf by the people when Moses failed to return from the mountain has a special significance. It is Israel's breaking of the Covenant, a failure to fulfil her identity as a people and as men, for those who fashion idols will be swallowed up by them. From this point this theme goes on to permeate the whole Bible, providing the mainstay of Jewish beliefs and passing on into the Christian religion.

On the eastern side of the Valley of Repose, almost at the mouth of the Wadi es Sheikh, the Bedouins have designated a small mosque on Gebel Harun, Mount Aaron, where the golden calf was supposed to have been erected (Exodus 32:1–8). For Islam, too, the Sinai is a symbol of the search for something more than an idol. Islam, which comprehends so well the concept of a single, invisible God, has marked the site of the sad, but always possible, return to idols wrought by man.

Land of Revelation

From the monastery of Saint Catherine set in the Wadi el Deir at the widening of the plain of El Raha, two paths lead to the top of Mount Sinai. The longer one, about two and a half hours, winds towards the east, leaving Gebel Katerìna on the left and laying before one a panoramic view of the whole Sinai region. The other route was used by thousands of pilgrims and one in particular, a fifth-century pilgrim, Eteria, has left us a description of it. The ascent is steep, marked out by an interminable flight of irregular steps, about four thousand in all, which the monks of the early centuries A.D. carved out of the rock.

The steps twist and wind in sharp, steep turns as the horizon widens and the monastery below appears like a small dot among the rocks. These steps have become perhaps the most meaningful symbol of the Sinai, of its history, the spirit which permeates its deserts, its mountains, and its sky. From the earliest days of Christianity they were climbed with great uncertainty by countless pilgrims who considered themselves the direct heirs of the people of Israel. We may speculate that if one had known a little about this fragment of the Sinai's history, that if the faith which drew those pilgrims up Mount Sinai had not died out, then there could never have been any dispute or ill will towards the People of the Covenant. And anti-Semitism, the blot on our history, would never have occurred.

Such was the similarity between the ascent of the great prophet of the Exodus and this new heavenward Exodus that a certain Giovanni, abbot of the monastery of Saint Catherine around the seventh century, wrote a work entitled *The Stairway to Paradise.* The stairway is the four thousand steps of Mount Sinai. Each step, each turning becomes a symbol of a struggle, a problem, a victory, a disappointment, a respite, or a liberation; in other words, an Exodus that never ends. This work has reached us with the author's full name, Giovanni Climaco. In Greek *climax* means "step." Traditionally the anchorites living in these places sometimes banded together to live as a family and they were called simply "the Climaxes," or the people of the steps. Of the many thousands only a few emerged from anonymity. All the others preferred to assume this collective name, which really means "those of the Exodus."

At one of the turnings there is a surprise. Almost between sky and earth stands a gate that opens on to the sky. This is the confessional where pilgrims stopped and fell to the ground to ask forgiveness. The words spoken to Moses were too harsh for them: "The place where you stand is holy!" Farther along is another gate, named after Saint Stephen—not the first deacon who died in Jerusalem but a hermit monk who lived on the mountain all his life preparing pilgrims for the final ascent.

About 800 steps before the summit, the path drops into a kind of natural amphitheatre, surrounded on all sides by gray and rose-colored granite. In the center are a spring, numerous small old churches in ruins, and some ancient cypresses. There is also a rock which indicates the place where Moses and his followers beheld God. This is also the place where Elijah saw God, not as Moses did, in the turbulence of a storm or in the burning of a fire, but in the sound of a gentle and restorative breeze (1 Kings 19:8–13).

From here begins the final climb to the top of the Mountain of Moses. The steps, worn by the wind, are now even steeper. For Islam, too, this last part of the ascent is fraught with religious tension and mystical emotion. Islam is irresistibly drawn when everything points towards a more pure, a more stark expectation, towards a God divested of any taint of human idolatry. Islam has also marked these places so that their value and immense importance will be remembered and passed on. The Bedouins have indicated a rock with two strange imprints, which are supposed to be the hoofmarks of the legendary horse ridden by Mohammed before ascending to heaven. Chapter VII of the Koran actually tells of a prophet, Saleh, whose tomb is believed to be in the Wadi es Sheikh. On the mountaintop is also a small mosque alongside the church, a sign of a great and continuous spiritual search, pure and sublime, such as that of Islam.

Everything appears as though suspended from time immemorial and for always against the final moment on which hangs the whole of the Exodus, the Covenant, the Sinai, history and man: the moment of God's visible manifestation.

Even if one does not share the beliefs of generations of believers, or accept what was said of the manifestation of God, the fact that a people like the Jews could have conceived of all this, imagined and said all this, in the way they have in their books, would be reason enough for our eternal gratitude.

After the last of the thousands of steps, one finally reaches the top of Mount Sinai. It is like a balcony jutting out into a void, an amazing accumulation of the most enormous blocks of granite that defy all explanation as to how they have held together for so long.

In the fourth century the monks built a small and modest chapel here on Mount Sinai. They had a feeling for proportion and modesty. From the summit the horizon appears like molten rock, from the Gulf of Suez to the west to the Gulf of Aqaba to the east, from the Red Sea to the south to the immense plateau of El Tîh to the north. On the eastern slope of the mountain is Moses's cave. Here Moses is supposed to have seen the face of God. Those words, recorded in the Book of Exodus, trembled with a nostalgia that embraces all possible nostalgias: "Show me they glory!" The reply is part of the basic contradiction that is written into all of the Sinai: "I will make all my goodness pass before you, and will proclaim before you my name 'The Lord'; . . . But you cannot see my face; for man shall not see me and live" (Exodus 33:19–23).

What happened above, what happened at the foot of this mountain, down there where we are now descending, in the center of the monastery, at the site of the burning bush, is something more than a religious fact (if such a thing can be said). Rabbi Israel Eugenio Zolli tried to say it in his memorable work: "the first word of a totally different logic, of an absolute beginning, an heroic form of life."

Land of Memory

Up here original creation was repeated, history began again. "What," asked Rabbi Heschel, "is the meaning of Moses's vision? Buddha under the tree of inspiration becomes aware of the precariousness of the world. Moses before the burning bush perceives its stability which defies destruction. He is astonished—the bush is in flames but is not consumed by the fire. We, too, walking in the desert sometimes reach the mountain of God from which we see the whole world. It is like a burning bush, alight with hate, envy, revenge and crimes; and yet it survives. History is like the burning bush. Even though each second is destined to disappear so that another may take its place, it is not destroyed." And the wise rabbi who lived so close to the horrors of recent history, which affected his people and himself, asks, "What gives meaning to history? The promise of a future. Without a promise history makes no sense. The meaning consists of a vision and an expectation, of living the future in the present. This is one of the gifts that the Bible offers to the world: a promise, a vision and a hope, provided that we retain in our memory the vision and the promise."

This is perhaps the fundamental point—and for us more so than anything else—before leaving the Sinai, that vision and promise become hope because we have the memory of them, because in that remote and vibrant repository which is the memory, mind, heart, and blood, vision and promise do not disappear. Then history has a meaning for the future.

If we look down from the top of Gebel Mûsa, we are seized by dizziness because of the height, the vastness, and the doubt: what will remain of all this?

There below, as we descend Gebel Mûsa, the pivotal point on which all of the Sinai depends, we catch sight of the monastery set into the miniscule oasis that we mentioned before tackling the many thousands of steps. If Gebel Mûsa is the pivotal point and the heart of the Sinai, the monastery of Saint Catherine is its "memory." Everything that happened in the Sinai, everything that was said, those who passed by here, the ancient Exodus and every other exodus—everything has been as though accumulated, continually relived and nourished between these walls.

The Emperor Justinian built the monastery and the basilica of Saint Catherine in 527. And there it has stood for fifteen centuries, its great granite walls marked with crosses and lambs.

For several hundred years after it was built, monks of every nationality and faith came to the monastery, where everyone could pray in the twenty chapels to be found along the narrow streets of this religious citadel—for that is in fact what the monastery of Saint Catherine is. An anonymous pilgrim who journeyed to the Sinai from Piacenza in the year 570 relates that at the monastery he met three abbots who spoke Greek, Latin, Coptic, and Syriac, and some interpreters for other languages. Even after the separation of Rome and Constantinople it was possible, or at least there was no problem, for Latins, Greeks, and the faithful of other sects to live together. Of this we have firm reports until after 1600.

The exterior of the monastery is extremely simple; the interior is a complicated network. We enter through an iron gate into a narrow, low passage shaped like pincers; then we pass through a second and a third gate. Self-defense was necessary against hungry hordes, passing Bedouins, and the Arab and Turkish invasions. Until a few decades ago the only way to enter the monastery was to be winched up in a net. Still visible today is the protruding gallery of the loggia that contained the winch. The German scholar Constantin Tischendorf, who reached the Sinai in 1844 and discovered the famous Bible manuscript *Codex Sinaiticus,* describes experienced being raised in a net within the monastery walls.

Once inside the walls, it is like the interior of a multicolored beehive. Innumerable structures in the most improbable styles and positions—verandas, galleries, porticos, stairways, cells for monks, rooms for guests, a picture gallery, library, church, mosque, minaret, bell tower. And yet all these disparate and not always beautiful parts seem to coalesce because of the genius for memory, a need to remember everything that is important and must not be forgotten. Here is the well where Moses is supposed to have met the seven daughters of Jethro; and here is a bush that is supposed to be a living reminder of the bush that burned without being consumed, so full of mystery, meaning, and promise. Justinian's architect designed the church like an atrium, leading to the little chapel of the burning bush in the apse, where one enters barefoot, as Moses did.

But now we come to the apse, and the mosaic with its pure vibrations of memory—wondrous, luminous and precise. Dating from the sixth or seventh century, the mosaic contains everything of the Sinai that one needs to carry with one, its few feet plumbing the Sinai's ancestral past and projecting into future memory.

It is more a metamorphosis than a transfiguration, which in Greek means "form that changes." The innocence of the solemn and hieratic Christ is lightly indicated by pale gold. Enclosed within a rhomboid, symbol of eternity, Christ emanates rays which suggest not the triumphant, but rather what is true, fervent and modest. Next to Christ are the two great figures of the Sinai epic, Moses and Elijah, rapt but not mannered, wondrous but not gesticulating. Placed around Christ are the three men of the vision of Tabor: Peter, James, and John, who are also rapt and wondrous, but more human, if you like. But we cannot actually say that the figures in this composition are placed "around" the metamorphosis. They have, rather, been absorbed, or perhaps projected outward; or perhaps they too have "changed form" while still remaining men. But Christ too, the central figure, is above all a man. What had happened in the meantime, from that day when Moses wanted to see God's face and it was not possible because Moses would have died? What had happened was that the distant hope of the Exodus became more concrete—the terrible God of Horeb who thundered amid lightning and red-hot clouds appeared with the face of man. And everything became pure, clear, peaceful light. Here in the heart of the Sinai, in place of the ancient God of the promise there is now the God of consolation and a future that continues to hold out hope, not by forsaking that promise but by taking new life from it. Tabor and Sinai, the beginning and the end, a continual recommencement of a past so incredibly rich that it is never finished. And the memory, that stabbing wound in the heart of history, a wound that never closes in this ardent heart of the world, the Sinai.

Perhaps the Sinai is not even a place. Or perhaps it is so intense, so bald and harsh, with all its historical impact, as to be purely a symbol. And the symbol is pure beauty; a timeless, placeless beauty. In the Sinai everything undergoes metamorphosis. Everything becomes beauty. Everything resolves itself in that "Face of Man." The Face is pure light, and the light is hope for the future submerged in the past of the Promise. As Al-Harizi sang:

> Many lands are attractive,
> But never has the eye beheld
> Beauty such as yours.
> I know not if the sky bows down to you,
> Or if you rise up to meet the sky.

It is good to leave the Sinai with this doubt about the sky and the land. "Do not jest with the mountain," the wise and good Rabbi Kotsk continues to murmur.

FERNANDO VITTORINO JOANNES

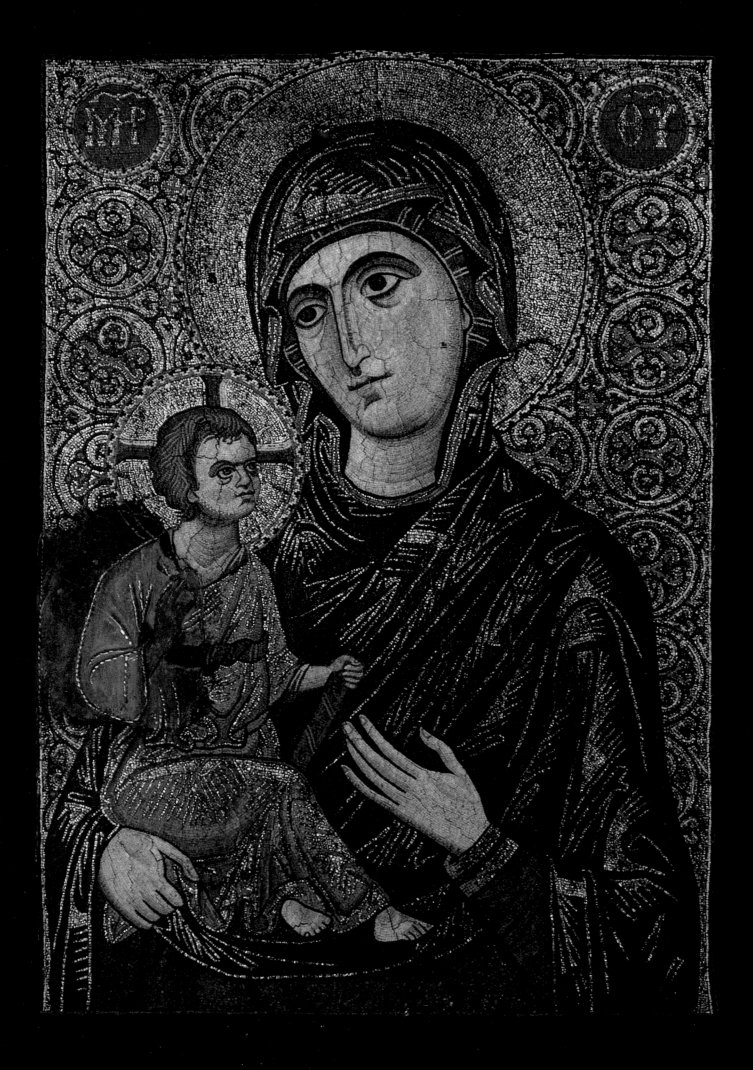

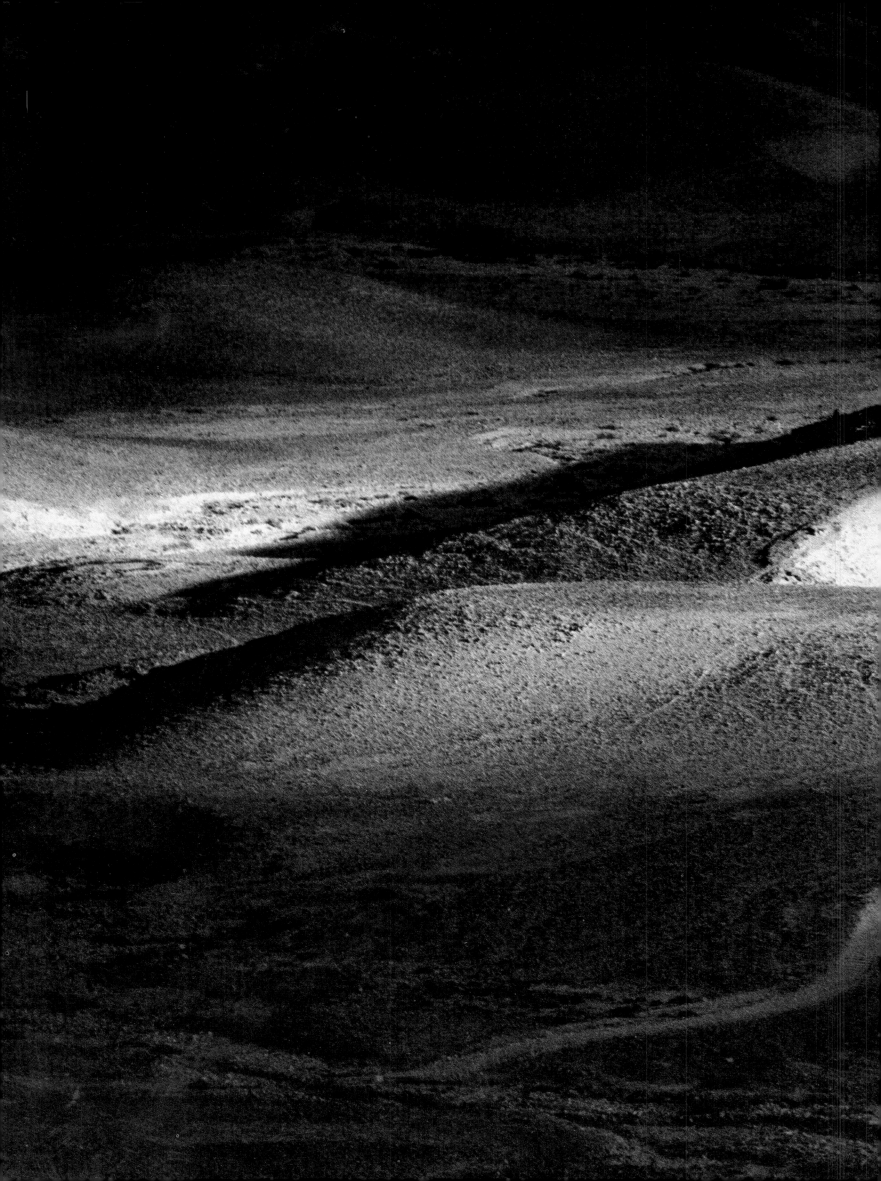

Travel Diary

Mount Nebo

The rainy season in Palestine and Jordan, which enjoy a Mediterranean climate, lasts four months and corresponds to the winter. It was during this period, on an icy morning in December, that we set out from Amman for Mount Nebo. The rain, accompanied by a fierce wind, never let up. It had transformed all the roads leading to Amman, which is set in a desert valley, into rivers of mud. We headed westward over inaccessible roads that were like rivers, anxious to reach the place where Moses had ended his life of travail. It was on Mount Nebo that his journey came to an end with the vision of the Promised Land, the land of Canaan, still before him:

> And Moses went up from the plains of Moab to Mount Nebo, to the top of Pisgah, which is opposite Jericho. And the Lord showed him all the land, Gilead as far as Dan, all Naphtali, the land of Ephraim and Manasseh, all the lands of Judah as far as the Western Sea, the Negeb, and the Plain, that is, the valley of Jericho the city of palm trees, as far as Zoar. And the Lord said to him, "This is the land of which I swore to Abraham, to Isaac, and to Jacob, 'I will give it to your descendants.' I have let you see it with your eyes, but you shall not go over there"
> —DEUTERONOMY 34:1

During their troubled journey, which began with the flight from Egypt and took them through innumerable stages as far as the plains of Moab, all those Hebrews who had been slaves in Egypt died, and only the second and third generations were at last able to reach the Promised Land. I, too, wanted to reach at least the top of Pisgah, on Mount Nebo, which commands a view of everything.

View of Mount Nebo
Studium Biblicum Archaeological Expedition, 1934

On leaving Amman, we travelled twelve and a half miles south and then headed west for Madaba, a city on the outskirts of Mount Nebo. The road seemed to descend continually as it wound through the hills like a ribbon. The torrential rain that had accompanied our departure from Amman continued unabated as sudden downpours, which prevented us from seeing anything, alternated with unexpected breaks in the heavy black rain clouds that revealed patches of blue sky, crossed by rainbows. But unfortunately these moments immediately ended with the rapid and continual movement of the clouds. This is desert rain.

At Madaba there were no signs for Mount Nebo, but everyone we asked for directions knew how to get there. We left the town and took an asphalt road full of holes, flanked on either side by rocky heights where the occasional old and misshapen olive tree provided the only touch of greenery to be seen in this season. But as we ad-

113

vanced we saw nothing that could be called a mountain. We continued westward along the descending road, and after about six miles we suddenly saw below us the narrow surface of the Dead Sea. We continued to descend for a bit and, after passing a Byzantine-style church and proceeding for another 320 feet, we found ourselves in front of a small rocky hill, at the foot of which a sign indicated that this was the mountain where Moses had died.

I could not have been more disappointed, for it was no more than an ordinary hill, a far cry from the imposing sight that I had imagined. I tried to console myself with the thought that we had come from the wrong side, considering that the road that brought us from Madaba was in descent the whole way. Or perhaps I had been deceived by the altitude of 2,631 feet indicated on the map, which convinced me that I would have to climb to that height, and by the dramatic description in the Old Testament. A rocky road led up the gentle slope to the top, a small ten-foot-square terrace. Gusts of icy wind greeted me as I got out of the car, but the view that lay before me was decidedly better than my expectations and compensated for my previous disappointment. In the distance one could see the Dead Sea, from north to south, winding across the desert until it took on the appearance of a green ribbon—the vegetation that grows along the banks of the Jordan; on the east bank of the river, the open country; on the other bank, the oasis of Jericho, more prominent with its darker shades of green. Jericho was the first city conquered after the death of Moses by the sons of Israel who, led by Joshua, crossed the Jordan. Beyond the Dead Sea and Jericho I could make out the wavy brown lines of the desert.

The reason why this magnificent view from the top of Mount Nebo is so fascinating is the particular conformation of the area. The Jordan Valley is below sea level, as are the banks of the Dead Sea (at least 1,300 feet), towards which the western slope of the Nebo descends precipitously with deep and craggy valleys. If you view Mount Nebo which rises 3,937 feet from the Dead Sea, it looks like an inaccessible peak. When the weather is fine one can probably see Jerusalem from up here and to the left, Bethlehem, set against the ridge of the mountains of Judah. Unfortunately the rain clouds gathering below prevented us from seeing them. Some rays of light filtered through the clouds, lending a gray tint to the landscape, which appeared to me like a "land of the dead," not at all like Canaan, that land of milk and honey. Aside from the green of the Jericho oasis and the east bank of the Jordan, there is nothing but desert, just like the deserts of Shur and Sin in which the sons of Israel had wandered. Before coming to Mount Nebo, I had gone all round the Israeli territory on the other bank of the Jordan (which I could see from Mount Nebo), but, with the exception of some oases and some cultivated fields recently planted by the Israelis, in this region one saw only shepherds moving from place to place in search of the scarce vegetation.

One day while the flock was grazing at the foot of Mount Sinai, Moses heard God's voice from "a flame of fire out of the midst of a bush," and learned that he had been chosen by the Lord to "bring forth out of Egypt . . . the sons of Israel" and thus free them from oppression. From that moment Moses became the intermediary between God and the people to whom he made known God's word, while he asked God to forgive the sons of Israel whose actions showed that they had not yet thrown off their heritage of slavery. After countless crises, which were always overcome, and after wandering for forty years, during the course of which Moses saw the death of all his companions with whom he had fled from Egypt—including his sister Miriam and his older brother Aaron—Moses finally succeeded in leading his people to this land.

What must have been his feelings on seeing the Promised Land, this man who alone was able to see it only after the struggles of such a long journey and at the end of his life? This question flashed through my mind as I was about to leave Mount Nebo. "Moses was a hundred and twenty years old when he died; his eye was not dim, nor his vitality reduced"; he was buried "in the valley in the land of Moab," but no one has ever found his burial place.

From Jerusalem to the Sinai

The first time you visit Israel you immediately notice of state-of-siege atmosphere. There is continual movement of tanks in readiness for battle on the road from Jerusalem to Jordan; signs indicate military zones where entry is forbidden; sandbags are piled up to fortify trenches. And yet despite all of these exercises by the Israeli army—and they are only exercises—the Bedouin pitch their tents and graze their sheep and goats, unmindful of what is happening around them.

When I reached the Dead Sea, the landscape seemed gloomy at first, perhaps because the desert of Judah is such a cheerless sight, an arid zone that extends beyond the west bank and receives very little rain. But this was only a momentary impres-

sion, because I immediately became enraptured by the astonishing contrast between the emerald green of the Dead Sea and the reddish color of the surrounding mountains. Another contrast that I found farther south at the Gulf of Eilat, almost at the border, was formed by the intense blue of the sea and the reddish mountains of Saudi Arabia, an amazing landscape at any hour of the day. Suddenly I saw a path completely bounded by barbed wire, alongside which was a sign in Hebrew, a language I do not know. After a fruitless search on my small map, I concluded that it was not on the map because the sign had been put up by the troops during the Six Day War.

There are in fact many reminders of that war in this area; for example, many areas with unreclaimed live ammunition are enclosed by barbed wire and entry is strictly forbidden. In order to take some photos we disobeyed the signs, and by balancing one on top of the other to form a human chain, managed to get over the barbed wire. On the road to the Negev the danger areas are not enclosed by barbed wire, but instead there are soldiers—who ordered us in no uncertain terms not to proceed, and a good thing too, considering how easily one could be blown up.

At last the road that runs through the entire valley, with its numerous incomprehensible signs, brings us to the Sinai Desert, a rocky plateau located at an altitude of more than 4,900 feet. The highest mountain of the group is Gebel Katherìna (8,668 feet) followed by Gebel Oasr Abbas Basha (7,818 feet) and Gebel Mûsa or, properly called, Sinai (7,362 feet) which stands alone in the middle of a plain. At the base of these mountains Bedouin tents are visible.

We attempted to ascend Mount Sinai by car,

but after a little over a mile, the car became stuck in the sand. After an hour of unsuccessful attempts to free it, using sticks as a lever, help arrived, in the form of some Israeli soldiers and Bedouin, who freed the car in a short time. Meanwhile the sun had set; in the fading light we were surrounded by silence. So we pitched our tent on the side of the road, which was completely covered by sand, and spent our first night in the Sinai. It was October but already terribly cold.

A Night at El Raha

The plain of El Raha extends to the north of Mount Sinai. It is regarded as the holy place where the sons of Israel, having fled from Egypt, stopped to receive the Tables of the Law. They had reached the Sinai three months after their flight from Egypt and stayed there for almost a year before resuming the journey that God had commanded them to make.

Most of the wadis that surround Mount Sinai are actually deep valleys, inaccessible and rocky. Only El Raha, with its gravel and sand, forms what we could call a gentle "plain" at the base of the mountain. According to the early Christians, the little hill located at the far corner of this plain at the foot of Mount Sinai, is the place where the Hebrew people waited anxiously for the return of Moses when he climbed to the top of the mountain to receive the Tables of the Law. Here too the golden calf was set up and worshipped.

The plain of El Raha is for the most part uninhabited. During the time we were there taking photographs of Mount Sinai and the surrounding area, we saw a few Bedouin families camped at the foot of the northern slope on the flat ground surrounded by rocks. Since the terrain in this area is composed of fine gravel, an ideal place to pitch one's tent, we made camp here as well. El Raha is situated nearly five thousand feet above sea level, which means that the winters are rather severe, like all the surrounding areas. At sunset the mercury falls rapidly and towards dawn is below freezing. A bucket of water left out at night will have formed a thick layer of ice by morning.

We finished supper and after a warming glass of whisky got straight into our sleeping bags. It was a freezing cold night and a strong wind was blowing. Gusts of wind laden with sand beat against our tent. As a precaution we drove the tent pegs in deeper; we then went to sleep at our usual hour of just after nine, but towards midnight we were awakened by the noise of a torrential rainstorm. The impact of the rain against the taut canvas produced a resounding din inside our tent. We hadn't met with such a violent storm since the downpour in the Negev.

In the desert, however, rain, being so infrequent, represents a truly divine gift; and in all likelihood it was the natural phenomena of the desert that led the shepherds to believe in the existence of a single God. In a life of uncertainty, moving continually from place to place in search of vegetation that grows after the sudden rains, a gift from God means, above all, rainfall.

In the desert the rain is never soft and silent, but arrives in a downpour without warning, accompanied by a stiff wind. First lightning appears from between the thick blanket of clouds that covers the sky in an instant, followed by thunder, and in that moment God's gift—anxiously awaited by everyone—arrives.

The Bedouin's god is merciful and inviolable; he draws near, with the thunder, to present his gift. But when faced with man's injustice, this god becomes angry and transforms the gift into an instrument of punishment.

The torrential rain that woke me and robbed me of my sleep did not last long. The wind also dropped and inside the tent there fell a deep silence, which was broken suddenly by an unaccountable noise: a rumbling followed by an echo, as though someone were grumbling or moaning softly. I soon realized that this was distant thunder which, reechoing between the steep mountains, had reached us here. After a little while I heard a new moan. As I lay there in the darkness, it seemed as though the thunder came from the sky and discharged itself into the innermost recesses of the earth. I never imagined that I would actually hear thunder at the foot of Mount Sinai, and I recalled the dramatic description in the Old Testament of God's appearance on that mountain: "On the morning of the third day there were thunders and lightnings, and a thick cloud upon the mountain, and a very loud trumpet blast, so that all the people who were in the camp trembled" (Exodus 19:16).

I crawled out of the tent to admire Mount Sinai illuminated by lightning. The wind had stopped but it was freezing cold. The sky was completely covered by black clouds and total darkness; one could make out only the dark outline of Mount Sinai against the clouds.

The next morning we rose before dawn. Large groups of cirrus clouds raced from west to east in the now-clear sky, while the peak of a nearby mountain was covered by thick clouds. It seemed that the moisture brought by the breezes had increased only in that spot. We drew near and then realized that a strong wind was blowing only in that place also, and that the clouds, pushed by the wind, were rising in the sky and disappearing, only to reappear and repeat the cycle again and again. I stayed there for a short time, fighting off the cold. The clouds rose like the smoke of a furnace; the whole mountain seemed to tremble.

Climbing Gebel Mûsa

Gebel Mûsa, as we know, means Mountain of Moses, a name given to commemorate Moses's receiving of the Tables of the Law from God. The mountain to the far north is called Gebel Ras es Safsaf and is 6,739 feet high.

The day after our arrival we decided to climb to the top of the mountain immediately. As we intended to stay the night up there, we took with us, aside from our photographic equipment, the tent, the sleeping bags, and food for twenty-four hours, planning to return the next day. We discovered, however, that it is impossible to pitch a tent on the rocky surface of a mountaintop, and that it is much better to seek refuge in one of the many natural grottoes.

Fortunately, as we climbed the long flight of four thousand steps leading to the top, we managed to avoid the intense light of the desert because this side is in the shade from the early hours of the afternoon. But climbing all those steps truly requires an enormous effort. Hot and tired, I drank far too much water and in a short time I began to perspire so much that I was forced to give up the climb.

Beginning again the next day, we noticed a decrepit hut where a hermit lives, surrounded by silence. Finally we reached the Gate of Saint Stephen, marking the end of the first part of the stairway. Before us appeared a large clearing overlooking the Sinai mountains. A group of cypresses stood alongside the chapel. Elijah's cave was inhabited by some hermits. A group of Israeli boys and girls were also resting in the clearing. Seeing a Bedouin offer bread and water to the pilgrims, we regretted having made our young assistant carry a flask of water. We resumed our climb and after three hours, as the first shadows fell on the western slope, we reached the summit. Here, according to tradition, Moses received the Tables of the Law. Here also a small church and a mosque have been built. To escape from the cold we entered the mosque and decided to spend the night there, although the place held no attraction. It was not very clean and in some places the paved floor had fallen in. The design faced Mecca, towards which Muslims direct their prayers. Despite our fatigue we had a look at the view before going to sleep. All we could see were the rocky mountains and here and there an abandoned eagle's nest where hermits now lived. The dark night had drawn in and only the whiteness of the church and the mosque stood out.

The intense cold forced us back to the mosque. Fortunately the cold night air had not yet penetrated within; in fact, we could still feel some of the heat absorbed by the walls during the day. We got into our sleeping bags and ate our frugal meal by the dim light filtering in from outside. One should not drink alcohol in a mosque, but considering that none of us were Muslim, we made a small exception to the rule. We managed to chat for a bit, but eventually sleep overtook us.

The Monastery of Saint Catherine

Standing on the eastern slope of Gebel Mûsa, the oldest monastery in the world is dedicated to Saint Catherine. At the beginning of the fourth century Christians were still the object of fierce persecution throughout the Roman Empire, and therefore many hermits and priests took refuge on Mount Sinai. It is said that Saint Helen, mother of the Emperor Constantine, came here on a visit between 325 and 330 and had built what is today the oldest part of the Chapel of the Burning Bush.

The monastery of Saint Catherine also includes a mosque, which may seem surprising. But there is an explanation. According to the legend, the troops of Sultan El-Haham (931–1021) had been ordered to destroy the monastery. But as there were no mosques in these parts where his men could pray, the sultan proposed a compromise. He would spare the monastery if the monks would build a mosque for his soldiers. And so it was. The mosque, which became doubly sacred, was also spared during the Crusades. It is no longer visited by pilgrims, only by the Bedouin who assist the monks.

Today there are about thirty monks living in the monastery, assisted by a group of Gebeliah Bedouin who live outside the monastery. In the tenth century the monks numbered 300 and in the fourteenth century 400; in the fifteenth century there was a dramatic drop in numbers, to barely thirty, and since then the number has remained fairly small: sixty in the seventeenth century, fifty in the eighteenth, and twenty-eight in 1871.

Today there are many pilgrims (besides tourists) coming to the Sinai, mainly groups of young Israelis who visit the places of the Exodus. The monks estimate that there are on average 100 visitors per day. During our stay we were lodged in the monastery, which from the earliest times has remained open to everyone; even though protected by thick walls and ditches, it has always offered hospitality to pilgrims. At four in the morning a bell calls the religious to prayer (only the monks, not the pilgrims) and they go to pray on the steps that they call "the road of Moses," which leads to Mount Sinai from behind the monastery. They spend many hours in prayer—from four to seven in the morning and from two to four in the afternoon. We would have liked to continue sleeping during morning prayers but were prevented by the Bedouin, who begin their duties of helping the monks at this time. Very little work goes into the preparation of the food, or at least the frugality of the meals suggests this. It is, however, immensely peaceful in this isolated place, particularly in winter.

The Bedouin

Nomadic Arabs are called Bedouin, *baadiya* in Arabic, which means "plain" or "desert," but probably has other meanings as well. Originally anyone who lived in tents in the desert was called by a very similar name in Arabic. In certain areas the common name for nomads is *shiva,* but in the Sinai even the sedentary Arabs are sometimes called Bedouin.

As their population increased their need for new pastures grew, and the Bedouin began to move more frequently and farther afield, advancing from Arabia as far as Egypt and the Sudan. Before the Suez Canal was opened to traffic, one Bedouin tribe, the Tiaheh, controlled the pilgrims' route to Mecca. They offered their services as guides to the pilgrim caravans—and often supplemented these earnings with raids. Now few in numbers, the Bedouin—who are Muslims—maintain a very closed community, which rejects most aspects of the modern world. They live mainly in inaccessible mountainous regions, in tents surrounded by fences made of simple sticks of wood.

The arable land of the oasis of Feiran provides a remarkable contrast with the surrounding land, which is barren and rocky with few grassy areas for sheep and goats to pasture. Here many Bedouin are able to have water within easy reach. The Israeli administration protects these tribes, which can draw water at any hour of the day from cisterns placed at regular distances along the side of the road. The Sinai Bedouin are divided into 400 tribes. The Touara live in the hilly district of the Gulf of Eilat; the Tiaheh in the desert area of El Tîh; the Tarrabin in the north of the Sinai, the region of the sand dunes, where Mediterranean civilization developed; the Hahuytat in the northwest, near the Gulf of Suez.

The largest tribe is the Touara, which is divided into six groups: the Soualkha, who live in the Wadi Feiran, the region west of the Sinai massif; the Aligat who inhabit the vicinity of Serabit el Khadim; the Muzeina, who live along the coast of the Gulf of Eilat; the Krasha, whose home is in the vicinity of the monastery of Saint Catherine in the Wadi es Seih; the Elad Said, who occupy the region of El Tur; and the Gebeliah, who live by the oasis of Feiran, also near the Saint Catherine monastery.

The Gebeliah came to this country in the sixth century from Valeria in Romania. They were sent by the Emperor Justinian to help the monks of Saint Catherine—a function they still fulfill today—and naturally they had to embrace the Christian religion. Subsequently, the Muslim faith of the other Bedouin infiltrated into their traditions, resulting in their conversion to Islam, although there are some Christians among them. When we told the Gebeliah that we also intended to photograph some other tribes, they replied scornfully that they were the only real Bedouin.

At the present time the two groups who assist and defend the monks are the Elad Said and the Es Soualkha.

During the Six Day War the Muzeina (who, as we said, inhabit the coast of the Gulf of Eilat, their home for the past 400 years or so), were engaged in contraband of arms and men with the Egyptians, and it is said that now they are selling drugs. The Bedouin live well in this area, due in part to the development of tourism. They have government protection and they live in rather comfortable houses that have basic modern conveniences with small gardens enclosed by barbed wire and a quantity of coconut trees.

As the Bedouin women took their goats and sheep to pasture, they saw us and, blushing with shame, tried to hide by crouching at the foot of the coconut palms. What should we have said? In this corner of the Sinai we really felt as though we were in another world.

The first part of our trip was over. We had finished our work in the Sinai and now had to retrace our footsteps across the Sinai desert, the wide Gulf of Eilat, the Dead Sea, the west bank of the Jordan. Once again we admired enthusiastically the various landscapes. When we reached Palestine it was already spring, a gentle spring with flowers of every color, and with young goats, born during the winter, grazing on the new grass. The spring mists hid the other bank of the Jordan and even Mount Nebo. Behind Jericho the Israeli tanks advanced amid the multicolored wildflowers. While we photographed the local inhabitants, the soldiers complained, or at least so it seemed. Every day in this country shots echo from valley to valley; young men with guns on their backs practice hand-to-hand combat.

We continued north along the west coast of the Jordan until we reached Lake Tiberias—passing, as it were, from the Old to the New Testament, for Christ lived here in Galilee. A moderate rain began to fall, benevolent for this season. This is a place of incomparable beauty: the lake, the hills, the gentle pastures where sheep and goats graze. Grapefruit and bananas are expertly cultivated in this area, and the air is scented with the delicate perfume of flowers; in spring, water from the melting snow cascades down the Lebanese mountains. In this garden where everything was flowering, butterflies flying and bees humming, it seemed almost impossible that on the other bank was a desert. But there remained signs of war, the Six Day War; after ten years there are still too many reminders. K.N.

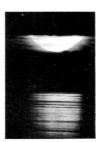

THE RED SEA. *Generally the sea is so calm that one does not even hear the sound of waves breaking on the shore. It is uncertain when the Red Sea, which separates the Sinai from the continent of Africa, was given its name, although the Greeks were the first to refer to it by these words. In the Bible it is called "the Sea of Reeds" in Hebrew.*

LITTLE BITTER LAKE. *"Then Moses stretched out his hand over the sea; and the Lord drove the sea back by a strong east wind all night, and made the sea dry land" (Exodus 14:21).*

CAPE OF RAS MUHAMMAD, RED SEA. *Off the western shore of Ras Muhammad in the Gulf of Suez is a coral reef. The water is not very deep here—no more than about 330 feet for a distance of about six miles—and there is no noise from these heavy seas. At low tide one can easily see the bottom.*

SEA OF REEDS, CAMELS BY THE SHORE. *This scene of camels walking along the shore is typical of this area, which is called by the natives "dry land in the middle of the sea." The domestic animals look for something to eat in the sandy soil where only weeds and suf, a kind of aquatic reed, grow.*

LITTLE BITTER LAKE. *According to tradition the miracle of the crossing of the Red Sea took place here. The event must have occurred farther south, some distance from the Mediterranean, in the region between Lake Timsah and the Gulf of Suez. Here, between modern Gebel Genneffe and Gebel Abu Hassan, three sites have been identified, Pi Hakhirot, Migdol, and Baal Zefon, where the Hebrews encamped (Exodus 14:2).*

CENTRAL-SOUTHERN SINAI. *Anyone who knows these parts is familiar with the strong hot southerly wind, the khamsin. It sends the clouds racing and picks up sand, which it disperses everywhere. We can go no farther: a barbed-wire fence encircles a mined field. The wind continues to blow on the peaceful dunes.*

WESTERN SINAI. *On the west coast of the Gulf of Suez, the mountains are separated from the sea by a desert belt: the desert of El Qâ'ah near Ras Muhammad, half of the Sin Desert, and the desert of Shur to the north, just below Suez. The landscape is typical of the Sahara.*

SUNSET ON MOUNT SINAI. *The sun sets on Mount Sinai. Moses remained on this mountain top for forty days and forty nights, as the Lord commanded, and he came down with the Tables of the Law.*

PLAIN OF EL RAHA. *Gebel Mûsa is clearly visible from the plain of El Raha. The Sinai massif extends for about two and a half miles from north to south with the tallest peak (8,668 feet) at the southernmost end. At the northern end is Ras es Safsaf (6,739 feet) on the left of the photograph. The monastery of Saint Catherine is hidden in the shadow of the mountain.*

GEBEL KATHERÎNA. *The view from the highest peak of the Sinai, Gebel Katherîna (8,668 feet) extends far to the north. The vast extent of these bare mountains resembles the surface of the moon. The view from here is magnificent: to the east the Gulf of Eilat, to the west the Gulf of Suez and the Egyptian mountains. Mount Sinai is more to the right, out of sight. It is February and the snow, which now remains only on the highest peaks, brings a chill to the air at sunset.*

BEDOUIN WOMEN IN THE PLAIN OF EL RAHA. *These bare and inhospitable mountains inspire thoughts of death, and this was probably the state of mind of the Jews when they passed through here during their exodus from Egypt. But these Bedouin were born here and for them there is no other world. What does the Sinai signify to them?*

VIEW FROM GEBEL ER-DEIR. *From Gebel Er-Deir we can see the monastery of Saint Catherine and the desert plain of El Raha, the "valley of repose." The sons of Israel stopped here for a year and were then obliged to leave, because they had offended God by making and worshipping the golden calf. In the early hours of the afternoon, the mountain shadows begin to move towards the monastery of Saint Catherine and rapidly envelop it.*

VALLEY OF THE WADI WATIR. *As we ascend the deep valley of the Wadi Watir, we unexpectedly come upon an expanse of water. It is said that until a few years ago there was another water source here, of which no trace remains. The torrential desert rains often carry away earth and sand, which then cover over such springs and cause them to disappear.*

MONASTERY OF SAINT CATHERINE. *The monastery of Saint Catherine is located at a height of 5,151 feet. The perimeter wall measures about 330 feet in length and about 230 in width. In the centre of the monastery on the first floor is the Church of the Transfiguration; to the left is the Chapel of the Burning Bush; on the left side just beyond a small grove is a little farm.*

THE EAST FACE OF MOUNT SINAI. *The rocks near the summit, worn smooth by the fierce winds that roar continually, have taken on a golden-brown color because of their granite composition. At the summit is a small white church, built by monks in the fourth century.*

MONASTERY OF SAINT CATHERINE. *The exterior is extremely simple, the interior is a complicated network of innumerable structures in the most improbable styles and positions: verandas, galleries, porticos, stairways, cells for monks, guest rooms. On the first floor the cupola of a fourteenth-century mosque contrasts curiously with the Church of the Transfiguration.*

SAINT CATHERINE, ICON OF MOSES. *This painting on wood, typical of the Sinai, depicts two different events from the life of Moses: the episode of the burning bush—which accounts for his youthful face—and the handing over of the Tables of the Law. All around are scenes from the life of Moses.*

SAINT CATHERINE, ICON OF THE MADONNA AND CHILD. *There are more than 2,000 icons in the monastery, of which about 100 are visible to the public. This type of representation of the Madonna and Child, which dates from the twelfth century and is executed in mosaic, is called* odigitria *("he who indicates the way") and is typical of Byzantine iconography.*

SAINT CATHERINE, APSE OF THE CHURCH OF THE TRANSFIGURATION. *This 1,400-year-old mosaic portrays a solemn and hieratic Christ enclosed within a rhomboid, symbol of eternity; beside him are the two great figures of the Exodus, Moses and Elijah; below are the three protagonists of the vision of Mount Tabor: Peter, James and John.*

GEBEL KATHERÎNA. *According to the legend, angels carried the body of Saint Catherine from Alexandria in Egypt to this mountain. The large cross that glows in the sunset is of more recent construction than the monastery and the steps. However, it definitely existed before the Napoleonic period.*

TOMB OF SHEIKH NABI SALIH. *The tomb of Sheik Nabi Salih is situated on the western side of the oasis of Feiran. The Bedouin and the Koran consider it the most sacred place in the Sinai, and the people living in the vicinity have built a cemetery around it. The photograph shows the Ottoman crescent flying from the cupola of the tomb.*

MONASTERY OF SAINT CATHERINE. *The visitor is astonished to find electric light in the monastery. It is supplied by a small generator. The nearest Bedouin village, more than four miles away, certainly does not have electric light.*

MONASTERY OF SAINT CATHERINE. *At the present time there are some thirty monks living in the monastery. It is forbidden to take photographs of them, but Father Sofronios agreed without too much difficulty. He has lived here for twenty-seven years, but for him the time has flown.*

MONASTERY OF SAINT CATHERINE. *Passing through the gate of the monastery cemetery, I am suddenly confronted by this figure wrapped in the* paludamentum *of the "grand monastic profession." His name was Stefan and it is said that his task was to build a stone stairway leading from the monastery across a mountain path to the top of Mount Sinai. Built during the first few centuries after the construction of the monastery, the stairway has approximately 4,000 steps.*

THE CEMETERY OF SAINT CATHERINE. *When the monks die, they are buried and then exhumed after a year; their bones are placed in a crypt like this one. This custom goes back to the time of the desert hermits, when the skulls were collected and placed in caves hollowed out of the rock.*

SAINT CATHERINE, CHAPEL OF THE BURNING BUSH. *Helen, mother of the Emperor Constantine, came to the Sinai between 325 and 330, and during her journey she wished to dedicate the chapel to the Virgin Mary. This wing of the monastery is the oldest part, and the early Christians are supposed to have met here. Sunlight comes through the chapel window only once a year.*

MONASTERY OF SAINT CATHERINE. *Few pilgrims or tourists visit the monastery in the middle of winter. Only a few monks are to be seen in these vast surroundings, assisted by as many Gebeliah Bedouin servants, who do not, however, live in the monastery. In the infinite calm of the evening only the cold beats against the bare walls.*

SOUTHERN SINAI. *A gust of wind sweeps the mountain clear of any detritus that has formed. In these arid zones the desert rain contains more detritus and sand than water.*

THE SUMMIT OF MOUNT SINAI. *On the summit of Mount Sinai a devout young Jew is praying. In his left hand he holds a narrow strip of leather, a tefillah, covered on both sides with passages from the Bible. On his forehead is placed a small leather box that contains pieces of parchment with writings from the Torah. On his head he wears the tallith, the prayer shawl.*

YOUNG GEBELIAH GIRL AND CHILD. *Although the Sinai Bedouin are very different physical types from the Sahara Bedouin, they have a similar division of labor. The women and children are responsible for many chores, such as drawing water from the well, taking the sheep and camels to pasture, and in general all of the heavy manual work. The men are principally engaged in trade.*

BEDOUIN WOMAN. *The highly original costumes of the Bedouin women include a belt and a veil, indispensable accessories. Shy and very reserved, this woman, when she noticed that I was going to take her photograph, quickly covered her face with the cloak that she wore on her head.*

WADI MAGHARAH. *At the time of the pharaohs the Sinai was a land rich in natural resources. This is the entrance of an extinct turquoise mine. The Egyptians have always greatly admired this stone, which symbolizes eternal life; and also—especially—the dark green topaz, which represents the resurrection. The mines of Magharah, which means "cave," extend for about five miles.*

GEBELIAH BEDOUIN. *The Gebeliah are descended from Christian families who were brought here by Justinian to serve at the monastery. They converted to Islam, but remained in the employ of the monks and as managers of the monastery property. Although the Sinai today belongs partly to Egypt and partly to Israel, the Gebeliah are directly responsible to the archbishop of the Sinai, who is an independent authority.*

WADI MAGHARAH. *The rocks at the entrance to the turquoise mines, which were once numerous in this area, are decorated with bas-reliefs illustrating the life and work of the miners. In this example an overseer is vigorously directing the slaves at their work.*

THE SINAI DESERT. *In the mornings an unexpected natural phenomenon occurs in this desert country: a very thick fog envelops everything so that one cannot see even a few feet ahead. This phenomenon has a simple explanation in that the Sinai is a narrow peninsula with a very irregular surface full of natural undulations. In Biblical times, however, these sudden changes were seen as the hand of God.*

SERABIT EL KHADIM. *A large fragment from a stele, with a dedication to a pharaoh, was found in an Egyptian temple dedicated to the Lady of Turquoise, the goddess of the mines. These remains, better preserved and much less sophisticated than those found in Egypt, have been valuable in studies of ancient Egyptian history.*

TABERA. *On a highland slightly over four miles from the oasis of El Qâ'ah stand these strange structures that recall the famous episode of the Exodus in which quails from heaven were carried on the sea winds in large numbers: ". . . and [they] gathered the quails; . . . and they spread them out for themselves all around the camp. While the meat was yet between their teeth, before it was consumed, the anger of the Lord was kindled against the people, and the Lord smote the people with a very great plague." (Numbers 11:33). This place became known as the "graveyard of greed."*

BEDOUIN LIFE. *The dull sound of stones being rubbed together as a woman grinds wheat—a timeless image. I was allowed to take this picture in the presence of the child's father, who never left my side and with each click of the camera urgently requested his payment.*

BEDOUIN WOMAN. *An unusual custom of the Sinai Bedouin is to attach gold and silver trinkets to the women's veils. In ancient times the women would wear all of their jewelry in order to cover as much of their faces as possible. This custom, however, is practiced solely by married women, and only the richest ones, for such trappings are very expensive.*

BEDOUIN LIFE. *Unleavened bread,* azimo, *being cooked over the fire. According to the Bible, when the sons of Israel fled from Egypt they left with such haste that they forgot to bring leavening. To commemorate the Exodus, Jews today still eat unleavened bread as part of a prayer of thanksgiving. This bread is in fact delicious, either hot when freshly baked, or cold when it has hardened.*

GEBEL SERBAL. *In the south, below the oasis of Feiran, one of the centres of monastic life in the Sinai, stands the mountain chain of Gebel Serbal; its highest peak is 6,791 feet. Its sharp notched outline, which seems quite ordinary in the brilliant sunlight, takes on a mysterious appearance in the evening. Here at Feiran the Israelites had their first taste of battle.*

OASIS OF FEIRAN. *The oasis of Feiran, "the fertile one," lies about 30 miles west of Mount Sinai. Hidden by great overhanging rocks, the pearl of the Sinai has ten fountains and an abundance of aromatic herbs, acacias, tamarisks, and hundred-year-old palms with twisted trunks.*

WADI ES SEIH, SOUTHERN SINAI. *A Bedouin rises early after a night in the shelter of the rocks. He has a few sips of tea for breakfast, then calmly loads his merchandise onto his camel's back and sets off. There is probably a small shop in the vicinity where the Bedouin buy their provisions.*

MOUNT SINAI. *There are many Bedouin tents around Mount Sinai. Overcoming their natural reserve, the Bedouin look with fascination at the large quantity of medicines we have with us. The children are as usual the first to approach us; and eventually even the women, seeing the camera and taking courage, approach.*

DESERT LANDSCAPE. *February. An early spring comes to the Sinai Desert. The splendor of the flowers contrasts with the harsh bare mountains in the background. The wind ruffles the flowers and in the profound silence there is nothing to remind one of the outside world.*

BEDOUIN LIFE. *Grazing is the principal activity of the Bedouin, and practically their only means of support. A Bedouin girl with her faithful dog puts the flock to pasture. She controls the animals with a stick and calls them with a strange, almost inhuman cry.*

PLATEAU OF EL TÎH. *In the middle of this desert lies a deep valley, formed from the detritus carried off by the wind. Thick vegetation grows at the valley bottom, and there is a pool of water and even a small waterfall. Unfortunately it is salty water and not drinkable. At sunset the sky and the sides of the valley are reflected in the water.*

BEDOUIN LIFE. *The heads of family meet inside a typical Bedouin tent. They love long conversations, and coffee is made on the hearths. When the tents are taken down, the hearths indicate to other nomads that this is a suitable site to set up camp.*

PLATEAU OF EL TÎH. *What a difference between these photographs and those on the preceding page, even though the two places are not very far apart. Lack of water has made the land dry, so that the ground appears parched and cracked. The Israelites passed through here during their exodus.*

THE BANKS OF THE JORDAN. *The young lambs born during the winter need milk and fodder for a long period, but by springtime they are strong enough to graze on the sparse vegetation under the shepherd's protective gaze.*

GEBEL HALAH. *At sunset a woman returns to camp by the side of Gebel Halah (2,927 feet), which extends towards the north, a short distance from the Mediterranean. This long mountain chain runs along the banks of a wadi, a dry riverbed that periodically fills with water and resembles a lake.*

BEDOUIN WOMAN. *The remarkable beauty of the Bedouin women is intrinsically related to their environment. These women lose much of their fascination if removed from their tribal life, with its customs and dress, where the visitor is accustomed to see them. They also tend to age rapidly, and lose their beauty when still very young.*

CAPE OF RAS MUHAMMAD. *At the southern tip of the Sinai Peninsula, the Cape of Ras Muhammad forms a magnificent bay. Offshore coral of extraordinary beauty gives the sea a dreamlike color, while the clear, pure water rises with the tide to cover the sandy seabed.*

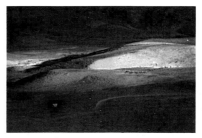

LAND OF JUDAEA. *A ray of light breaks through the clouds and falls on a herd of goats. To the west of the Dead Sea stretch the rolling hills of Judaea, which figured significantly in the accounts of the patriarchs.*

VICINITY OF EL ARISH. *This once peaceful land was a battleground for the Six-Day War, during which the Egyptian army was destroyed by Israeli tanks. A trainload of ammunition blew up with a tremendous explosion. Everywhere unexploded shells are buried in the sand, which after ten years still holds captive the town's railway line.*

BANKS OF THE JORDAN. *Unlike the Sinai Bedouin, who live in tribes of small numbers, the Bedouin of Jordan, when necessary, live in groups of more than one hundred, divided among ten or so tents. They tend to be much less nomadic and often these camps become permanent. The clearest indication of this is a nearby well of cement construction.*

JERICHO. *In the words of Moses, Jericho means "city of palms." Fortified against an attack by the Israelites, Jericho was nonetheless conquered by Joshua. "So the people shouted, and the trumpets were blown. As soon as the people heard the sound of the trumpet, the people raised a great shout. . . ."* (Joshua 6:20.)

LAKE OF TIBERIAS. *The wild flowers are watered by the melting snows that cascade down from the Lebanese mountains and flow into Lake Tiberias. There is no more beautiful sight in all the district than the neighboring mountains with their verdant meadows. After so much desert this is truly the Promised Land.*

JERICHO. *This now demolished village was built between 1945 and 1948, outside the old city, to house 10,000 Palestinian refugees who fled from the approaching Israeli troops. Most of the population later found refuge in Jordan, and now the village is completely abandoned.*

SODOM. *Along the Dead Sea shore can be found pillar after pillar of salt, but they only measure from about eight inches to three to six or seven feet in height. This is where Sodom and Gomorrah once stood, before God in his wrath destroyed them. These salt formations provided the inspiration for the biblical episode of Lot's wife, who was turned into a pillar of salt.*

ACACIA TREE. *Acacias with small leaves and long sharp thorns flower abundantly in the oases. The Ark of the Covenant, in which Moses placed the Tables of the Law, was made from the wood of the acacia tree, commonly found in the Sinai.*

DEAD SEA. *Only the mouth of the Jordan flows into this landlocked sea; its salt content is exceptionally high. Its name derives from the fact that no living creature can survive in its waters. Fish that enter from the Jordan die immediately. Legend has it that Sodom and Gomorrah, the cities cursed by God, are buried here under the salt.*

VICINITY OF THE TIRZA RIVER. *The Tirza River, a tributary of the Jordan, is located thirty-one miles from Jericho. The surrounding land is very fertile and has a large number of canals. In this region the land is green and rich with vegetation only in the winter.*

VICINITY OF THE TIRZA RIVER. *According to the Bible and Christian tradition, there is no greater sacrificial offering than the lamb. The reason for this is very simple. Sheep farming is everything for the inhabitants of the Sinai: the sheep gives milk, wool, and meat. As it is their most precious possession, it has the greatest value as a sacrifice to God.*

Acknowledgements

Having completed my work, I wish to express my most sincere thanks to the many people who helped to make this book possible. I wish to thank in particular the Israeli military who allowed me on occasion to go into prohibited areas to photograph and better observe certain places; the members of the Nature Reserve Society of Israel; the monks of the monastery of Saint Catherine; Father Michele Piccirillo, director of the Studium Biblicum of the Franciscanum Museum of Jerusalem; Father Damianos, archbishop of the Sinai; Mr. Inditzky of Tel Aviv; my efficient assistant Yoshihiro Umetsu.

Finally, my warmest thanks to Mr. Tom Mori, Mr. Tohru Tanabe of Heibonsha Publishers, and Mr. Enzo Angelucci of Mondadori Publishing Company, who have made possible the international publication of this book.

K.N.